ENGLISH/SPANISH EDITION

W9-BLO-762

The Oxford Picture Dictionary

for the

CONTENT AREAS

Dorothy Kauffman
Gary Apple

OXFORD

UNIVERSITY PRESS

Oxford University Press
198 Madison Avenue
New York, NY 10016 USA

Great Clarendon Street
Oxford OX2 6DP England

Oxford New York
Auckland Bangkok Buenos Aires Cape Town Chennai
Dar es Salaam Delhi Hong Kong Istanbul Karachi Kolkata
Kuala Lumpur Madrid Melbourne Mexico City Mumbai Nairobi
São Paulo Shanghai Taipei Tokyo Toronto

OXFORD is a trademark of Oxford University Press.

ISBN 0-19-436153-5

Editorial Manager: Shelagh Speers
Project Editor: Charles Flynn Hirsch
Associate Editor: Stephen McGroarty
Editorial Assistants: Francesca Merlini, Peter Graham
Senior Production Editor: Paul B. Philips
Elementary Design Manager: Doris Chen Pinzon
Designer: Nona Reuter
Art Buyers: Alex Rockafeller: Paula Radding, Bill SMITH Studies
Production Manager: Abram Hall

Translation and Production by Editorial Options, Inc.

Cover design by None Reuter & Doris Chen Pinzon

Illustrations by Wendy Wassink Ackison, Carin Baker,
Kim Bames/Artworks New York, S. Talmond Brown.
Rob Burman, Dan Burr, Sai Catalano, Mary Chandler,
Mona Diane Conner, Dom D'Andrea. Grace DeVito, Jim Effler
c/o American Artists Rep. Inc., Russell Farrell c/o American
Artists Rep. Inc., Jeff Foster, Michael Garland, John Paul
Genzo, GeoSystems Global Corporation, David Henderson,
Aleta Jenks, Uldis Klavins, Jerry Lofaro c/o American Artists
Rep. Inc., Alan Male c/o American Artists Rep. Inc.,
Lee MacLeod, William Maughan, Tom Newsom, Larry Salk, Bill
Schmidt, Wendy Smith-Griswold, Tim Spransy,
Taylor Stamper, Shannon Stimweis, Ron Tanovitz

Printing (last digit): 10 9 8 7 6 5 4

Printed in China

Oxford University Press is a department of the University of
Oxford. It furthers the University's objective of excellence in
research, scholarship, and education by publishing worldwide

PREFACE

The Oxford Picture Dictionary for the Content Areas is designed for elementary school students who are learning English. The Dictionary presents over 1,500 words drawn from the content areas of social studies, history, science, and math. The words are presented in full-page illustrations that place each word in context.

Dictionary Organization

- **Units and Topics.** The Dictionary is divided into eight thematic units. Each unit is divided into separate topics. The first unit relates to ESL students' experiences in their schools, families, and communities. The next seven units focus on the content areas of social studies, history, science, and math. Each topic has a full-page illustration which appears on the right-hand page. The left-hand page features the content words, each accompanied by a small picture to call out the word in the illustration. These "callouts" help students isolate each word as they search for it in the context of the illustration. Individual topics generally feature 12 to 20 callouts.

- **Appendix.** The appendix includes vocabulary and illustrations for numbers, time, money, colors, a calendar, food, clothing, and a map of the world.

- **Word List.** An index of words follows the appendix. The callout words appear in black. The key words that appear in a topic's title or within an illustration appear in pink.

Using the Dictionary as a Program

The Dictionary can be used by itself to supplement existing ESL programs, or it can be used with its additional components to make a suitable English language curriculum. These components include:

- *Teacher's Book*
- *Reproducibles Collection*
- *Workbook*
- *Cassettes*
- *Wall Charts*
- *Transparencies*

The *Reproducibles Collection* is a boxed set of four books:

- *Word and Picture Cards*
- *Worksheets*
- *Content Readings*
- *Content Chants*

The *Content Readings* explain the topics as they are depicted in the illustrations. *Content Chants* provide further practice in language and content. Readings of the *Dictionary, Content Readings,* and *Content Chants* are available on cassettes. The *Picture Dictionary* is available in both monolingual and bilingual editions.

PREFACIO

The Oxford Picture Dictionary for the Content Areas (*El Diccionario Ilustrado Oxford de las áreas de contenido*) está diseñado para estudiantes de primaria que están estudiando inglés. El Diccionario contiene cerca de 1,500 palabras que fueron extraídas de las áreas de estudios sociales, historia, ciencias y matemáticas. Las palabras se presentan en contexto en páginas minuciosamente ilustradas.

Organización del Diccionario

- **Unidades y temas.** El Diccionario está dividido en ocho unidades temáticas. Cada unidad está dividida en distintos temas. La primera unidad trata de las experiencias que los estudiantes de ESL tienen en la escuela, en la familia y en la comunidad. Las siete unidades restantes se centran en las áreas de contenido de estudios sociales, historia, ciencias y matemáticas. Cada tema viene acompañado de una ilustración en la página derecha, y una lista de las palabras en la página izquierda; cada palabra lleva un pequeño dibujo que corresponde a la ilustración. Estas referencias ayudan al estudiante a aislar cada palabra mientras la busca en el contexto de la ilustración grande. En general, cada tema tiene entre 12 y 20 palabras de referencia.

- **Apéndice.** El apéndice incluye vocabulario e ilustraciones de números, tiempo, dinero, colores, el calendario, alimentos, ropa y un mapa mundial.

- **Lista de palabras.** Después del apéndice hay un índice de palabras. Las palabras de referencia aparecen en letra negra. Las palabras que forman parte del título de un tema o de una ilustración, aparecen en letra rosa.

El Diccionario como programa

El Diccionario se puede usar como complemento de los programas de ESL o con sus componentes adicionales, para presentar un currículo de inglés adecuado. Los componentes son:

- *Teacher's Book*
- *Reproducibles Collection*
- *Workbook*
- *Cassettes*
- *Wall Charts*
- *Transparencies*

Reproducibles Collection es un paquete de cuatro libros:

- *Word and Picture Cards*
- *Worksheets*
- *Content Readings*
- *Content Chants*

En *Content Readings* se describen los temas tal como aparecen en las ilustraciones. Los *Content Chants* brindan práctica adicional del lenguaje y del contenido. El texto del Diccionario, de las *Content Readings* y de los *Content Chants* está disponible en las *Cassettes*. *The Oxford Picture Dictionary for the Content Areas* está disponible en versión monolingüe y en versión bilingüe.

TABLE OF CONTENTS
Contenido

THE CLASSROOM
El salón de clases

1. student
estudiante

2. teacher
maestro

3. desk
escritorio

4. chair
silla

5. table
mesa

6. book
libro

7. computer
computadora

8. pencil
lápiz

9. pen
pluma

10. crayon
creyón

11. paper
papel

12. notebook
cuaderno

13. ruler
regla

14. chalkboard
pizarrón

15. bulletin board
tablero de anuncios

16. map
mapa

17. overhead projector
proyector de transparencias

18. pencil sharpener
sacapuntas

19. cassette player
grabadora

20. wastebasket
cesto de basura

THE SCHOOL
La escuela

 **1. playground**
patio de recreo

 **2. office**
oficina

 **3. principal**
directora

 **4. secretary**
secretaria/o

 **5. cafeteria**
cafetería

 6. gym
gimnasio

 **7. coach**
entrenadora

 **8. hall**
pasillo

 **9. water fountain**
bebedero

 10. locker
armario

 11. boys room
vestidor de hombres

 12. girls room
vestidor de mujeres

 13. custodian
personal de intendencia

 **14. auditorium**
auditorio

 **15. stairs**
escaleras

 **16. library**
biblioteca

 **17. librarian**
bibliotecario

 **18. media center**
centro de multimedia

READ
EXIT
EXIT

THE HOUSE
La casa

1. **porch**
porche

2. **window**
ventana

3. **door**
puerta

4. **basement**
sótano

5. **kitchen**
cocina

6. **cupboard**
alacena

7. **living room**
sala

8. **floor**
piso

9. **bathroom**
baño

10. **toilet**
excusado

11. **sink**
lavabo

12. **bathtub**
bañera

13. **shower**
regadera

14. **bedroom**
recámara

15. **closet**
armario

16. **wall**
pared

17. **ceiling**
techo

18. **attic**
ático

19. **roof**
techo

20. **chimney**
chimenea

THE FAMILY
La familia

1. grandparents
abuelos

7. baby
bebé

2. grandmother
abuela

8. sister
hermana

3. grandfather
abuelo

9. brother
hermano

4. parents
padres

10. aunt
tía

5. mother
madre

11. uncle
tío

6. father
padre

12. cousins
primos

THE CITY
La ciudad

1. restaurant
restaurante

2. newsstand
puesto de periódicos

3. hotel
hotel

4. post office
correo

5. department store
tienda de departamentos

6. office building
edificio de oficinas

7. apartment building
edificio de apartamentos

8. church
iglesia

9. mosque
mezquita

10. temple
templo

11. parking garage
estacionamiento

12. bank
banco

13. movie theater
cine

14. police station
estación de policía

15. subway
metro

16. bus
autobús

17. taxi
taxi

18. garbage truck
camión de la basura

19. helicopter
helicóptero

20. traffic light
semáforo

THE SUBURBS
Los barrios periféricos

 1. **street**
calle

 2. **sidewalk**
acera

 3. **crosswalk**
paso peatonal

 4. **corner**
esquina

 5. **block**
cuadra

 6. **stop sign**
señal de alto

 7. **mailbox**
buzón

 8. **fire hydrant**
hidrante

 9. **yard**
patio

 10. **garden**
jardín

 11. **garage**
cochera

 12. **driveway**
entrada de autos

 13. **park**
parque

 14. **swimming pool**
alberca

 15. **gas station**
gasolinera

 16. **van**
camioneta

 17. **car**
coche

 18. **motorcycle**
motocicleta

 19. **bicycle**
bicicleta

 20. **basketball**
básquetbol

THE COUNTRY
El 'campo

 **1. farm**
granja

 2. barn
granero

 **3. silo**
silo

 **4. path**
camino

 **5. fence**
cerca

 **6. chicken coop**
gallinero

 **7. orchard**
huerto

 **8. pasture**
prado

 **9. pond**
estanque

 **10. woods**
bosque

 **11. hills**
colinas

 **12. field**
campo

 **13. road**
carretera

 14. stream
arroyo

 **15. bridge**
puente

 **16. airplane**
avión

 **17. train**
tren

 **18. truck**
camión

 **19. tractor**
tractor

 **20. wagon**
carretón

THE HOSPITAL
El hospital

 1. **patient**
paciente

 2. **doctor**
médico

 3. **examination table**
mesa de auscultación

 4. **bandage**
venda

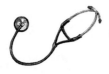 5. **stethoscope**
estetoscopio

 6. **thermometer**
termómetro

 7. **medicine**
medicina

 8. **X ray**
rayos X

 9. **nurse**
enfermera

 10. **crutches**
muletas

 11. **cast**
yeso

 12. **wheelchair**
silla de ruedas

 13. **bed**
cama

 14. **pillow**
almohada

 15. **blanket**
cobija

 16. **ambulance**
ambulancia

 17. **paramedic**
paramédico

 18. **stretcher**
camilla

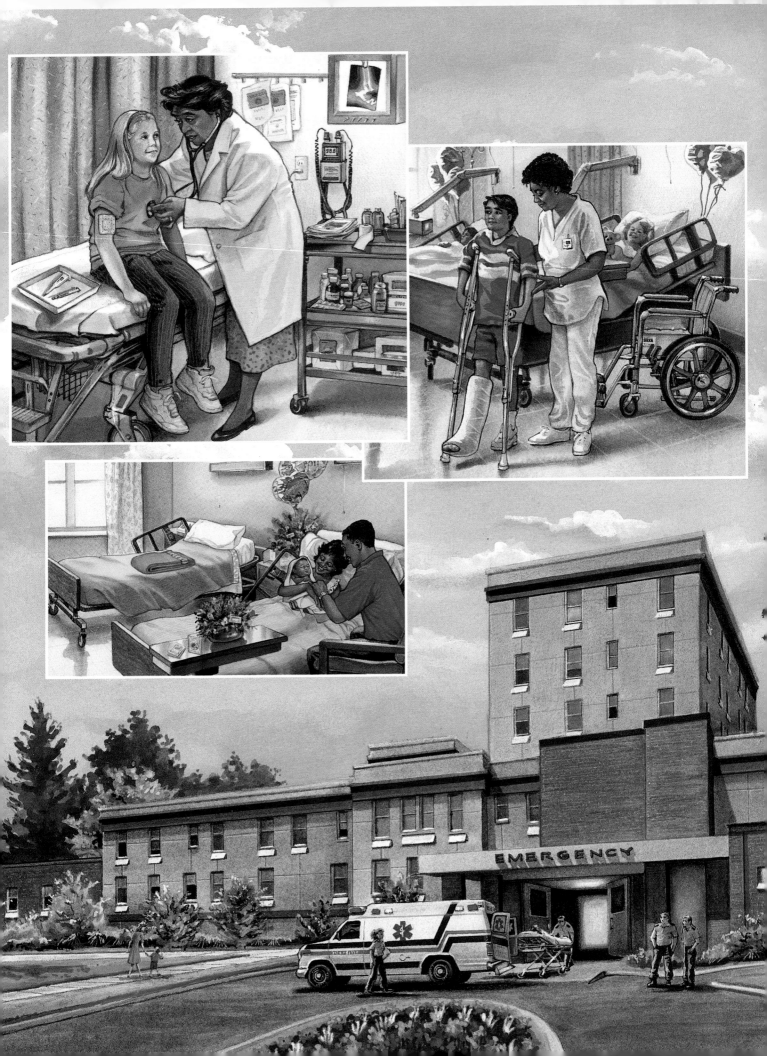

EMERGENCY

PEOPLE AT WORK
Oficios

 1. **construction worker**
trabajador de
la construcción

 2. **electrician**
electricista

 3. **carpenter**
carpintero

 4. **mail carrier**
cartero

 5. **firefighter**
bombero

6. **police officer**
policía

 7. **mechanic**
mecánico

8. **messenger**
mensajero

9. **musician**
músico

 10. **painter**
pintor

 11. **computer operator**
programador
de computadoras

 12. **writer**
escritor

 13. **dentist**
dentista

 14. **dental assistant**
ayudante de
dentista

 15. **hairdresser**
peluquera

 16. **plumber**
plomero

 17. **pharmacist**
farmacéutica

 18. **salesperson**
vendedor

FIRE STATION Nº 67

THE UNITED STATES
Los Estados Unidos

TOPIC
10

AL Alabama	IN Indiana	NV Nevada	TN Tennessee
AK Alaska	IA Iowa	NH New Hampshire	TX Texas
AZ Arizona	KS Kansas	NJ New Jersey	UT Utah
AR Arkansas	KY Kentucky	NM New Mexico	VT Vermont
CA California	LA Louisiana	NY New York	VA Virginia
CO Colorado	ME Maine	NC North Carolina	WA Washington
CT Connecticut	MD Maryland	ND North Dakota	WV West Virginia
DE Delaware	MA Massachusetts	OH Ohio	WI Wisconsin
DC District of Columbia	MI Michigan	OK Oklahoma	WY Wyoming
FL Florida	MN Minnesota	OR Oregon	GU Guam
GA Georgia	MS Mississippi	PA Pennsylvania	AS American Samoa
HI Hawaii	MO Missouri	RI Rhode Island	VI U.S. Virgin Islands
ID Idaho	MT Montana	SC South Carolina	PR Puerto Rico
IL Illinois	NE Nebraska	SD South Dakota	

The United States
Estados Unidos de Norteamérica

AK

N
W · E
S

WA
MT
ND
OR
ID
MN
WI
MI
SD
WY
IA
NY
PA
NV
UT
CO
NE
IL
IN
OH
WV
VA
CA
KS
MO
KY
NC
TN
SC
OK
AR
MS
AL
GA
NM
AZ
TX
LA
FL

ME
VT
NH
MA
RI
NJ
CT
DE
MD
DC

HI

U.S. Territories
Territorios de EE.UU.

GU

AS

VI

PR

THE NORTHEAST
Communication and Finance
El Noreste: Comunicaciones y finanzas

 1. **stock market**
mercado de valores

 2. **stocks and bonds**
acciones y bonos

 3. **businessperson**
empresario

 4. **newspaper**
periódico

 5. **magazine**
revista

 6. **buy**
comprar

 7. **sell**
vender

8. **headline**
titular

 9. **advertisement**
anuncio

 10. **studio**
estudio

 11. **newscaster**
comentarista

 12. **television**
televisión

 13. **radio**
radio

 14. **telephone**
teléfono

 15. **satellite**
satélite

 16. **Statue of Liberty**
Estatua de la Libertad

 17. **Liberty Bell**
Campana de la Libertad

 18. **The White House**
la Casa Blanca

GREETINGS FROM THE NORTHEAST!

THE SOUTH
Food Processing and Manufacturing
El Sur: Procesado de alimentos y manufacturación

1. **sugarcane**
caña de azúcar

2. **cotton**
algodón

3. **rice**
arroz

4. **crop**
cosecha

5. **sugar**
azúcar

6. **factory**
fábrica

7. **worker**
trabajador

8. **assembly line**
linea de ensamblaje

9. **lumber**
madera

10. **cloth**
tela

11. **thread**
hilo

12. **furniture**
muebles

13. **raw materials**
materias primas

14. **goods**
productos

15. **port**
puerto

16. **plantation**
plantación

17. **Mississippi River**
Río Mississippi

18. **Kennedy Space Center**
Centro Espacial Kennedy

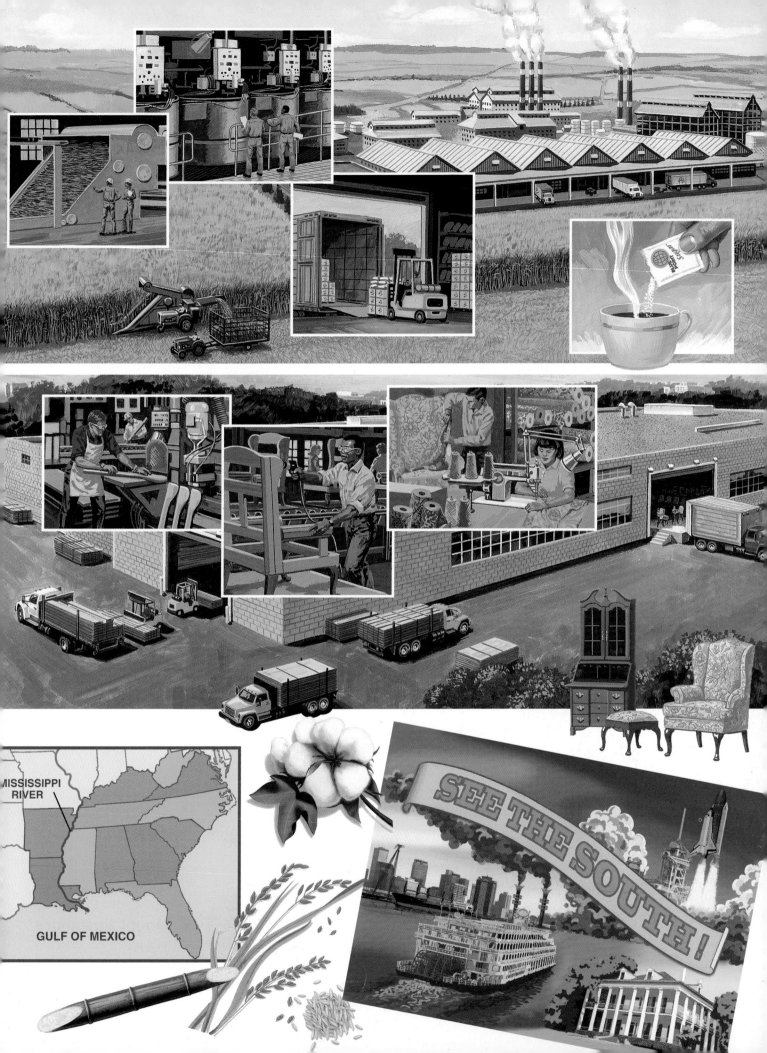

MISSISSIPPI RIVER

GULF OF MEXICO

SEE THE SOUTH!

THE MIDWEST
Agriculture and Dairy Farming
El Medio Oeste: Agricultura y la industria lechera

 **1. dairy barn**
granja lechera

 **2. cattle**
ganado

 **3. farmhouse**
hacienda

 **4. plant**
planta

 **5. harvest**
cosechar

 **6. plow**
arado

 **7. combine**
segadora

 **8. hay**
heno

 **9. wheat**
trigo

 **10. soybeans**
soya

 **11. corn**
maíz

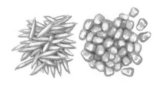 **12. grain**
grano

 **13. grain elevator**
elevador de granos

 **14. Great Lakes**
Grandes Lagos

 **15. Great Plains**
Grandes Llanuras

 **16. Mount Rushmore**
Monte Rushmore

TOPIC
13

COME TO THE MIDWEST!

THE WEST
Mining and Ranching
El Oeste: Minería y ganadería

1. open pit
cantera

2. mine
mina

3. ore
mena

4. minerals
minerales

5. ranch
rancho

6. livestock
ganado

7. corral
corral

8. cowgirl
vaquera

9. cowboy
vaquero

10. buffalo
bisonte

11. herd
rebaño

12. graze
pastorear

13. Rocky Mountains
Montañas Rocosas

14. peak
cima

15. Continental Divide
Divisoria Continental

16. rodeo
rodeo

17. Yellowstone National Park
Parque Nacional de Yellowstone

18. Old Faithful
Old Faithful

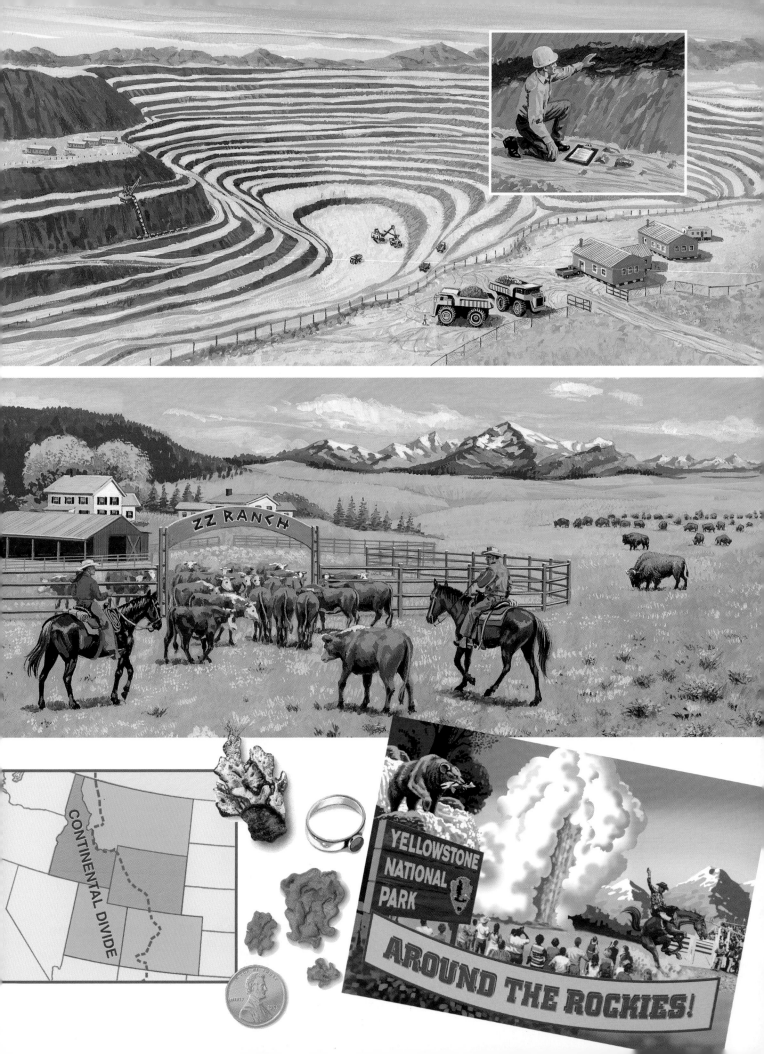

THE NORTHWEST
Forestry and Fishing
El Noroeste: Silvicultura y pesca

 **1. forest**
bosque

 **2. logging**
tala

 3. lumberjack
leñador

 **4. chain saw**
sierra de cadena

 **5. redwood**
secoya

 6. pine
pino

 **7. timber**
árboles maderables

 **8. sawmill**
aserradero

 **9. wood**
madera

 **10. sawdust**
aserrín

 **11. fish**
pez

 **12. cannery**
fábrica de conservas

 **13. boat**
bote

 **14. net**
red

 **15. rainfall**
precipitación pluvial

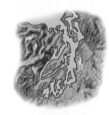 **16. Puget Sound**
Puget Sound

 **17. Space Needle**
Aguja Espacial

 **18. Alaska Pipeline**
Oleoducto de Alaska

VISIT THE NORTHWEST!

THE SOUTHWEST
Managing Natural Resources
El Suroeste: Explotación de los recursos naturales

1. well
pozo

2. oil
petróleo

3. natural gas
gas natural

4. drill
taladro

5. refinery
refinería

6. pipeline
oleoducto

7. tank
tanque

8. gasoline
gasolina

9. water storage
depósito de agua,

10. dam
represa

11. reservoir
reserva

12. irrigation canal
canal de irrigación

13. hydroelectric plant
planta hidroeléctrica

14. electricity
electricidad

15. Grand Canyon
Gran Cañón

16. cactus
cacto

CALIFORNIA
US
66

THE BEAUTIFUL SOUTHWEST!

WORLD OIL

Hiking Trails

Flora & Fa
Pinon pine

THE WEST COAST AND PACIFIC
Technology, Tourism, and Entertainment
La Costa Oeste y el Pacífico: Tecnología, turismo y entretenimiento

TOPIC 17

1. filmmaking
cinematografía

2. actor
actor

3. actress
actriz

4. director
director

5. script
guión

6. camera
cámara

7. set
escenario

8. fiber optics
fibras ópticas

9. laser
rayo láser

10. microchip
microchip

11. resort
centro turístico

12. tourist
turista

13. surfing
hacer surf

14. freeway
autopista

15. shopping mall
centro comercial

16. Golden Gate Bridge
puente Golden Gate

CANADA AND MEXICO

Canadá y México

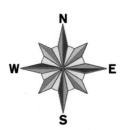

1. **compass rose**
rosa de los vientos

7. **state**
estado

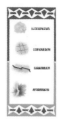

2. **legend**
leyenda

8. **capital**
capital

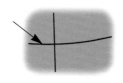

3. **latitude**
latitud

9. **money**
dinero

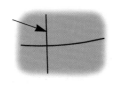

4. **longitude**
longitud

10. **totem pole**
tótem

5. **national border**
frontera

11. **pyramid**
pirámide

6. **province**
provincia

12. **silver**
plata

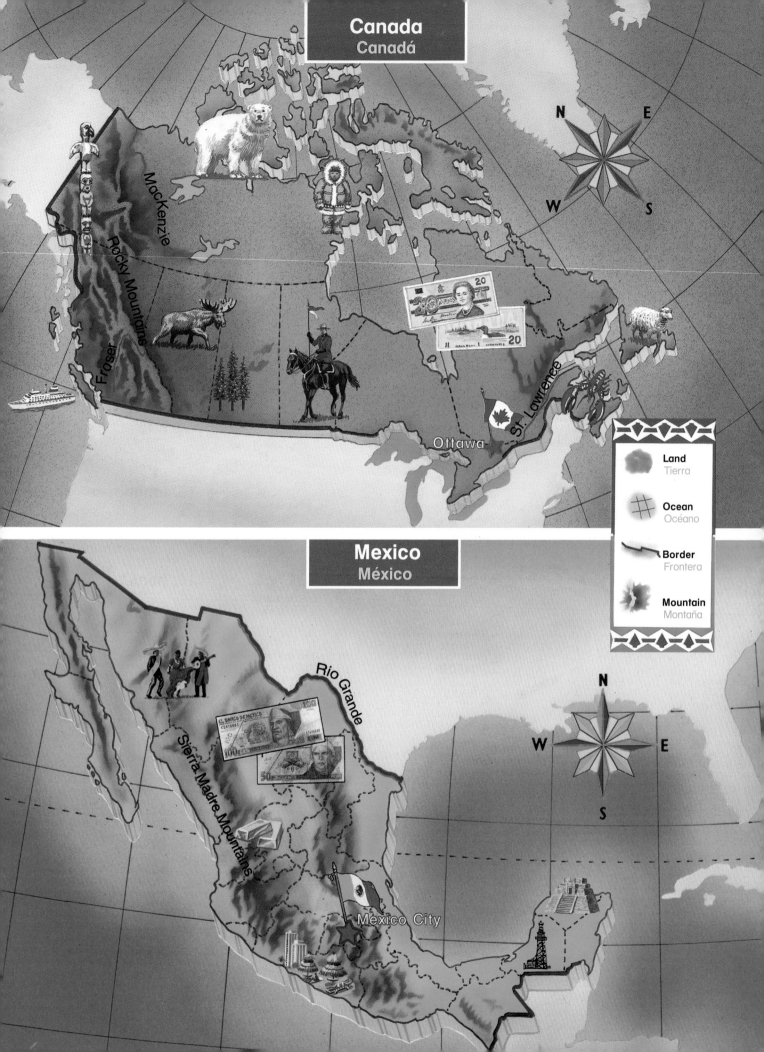

Canada
Canadá

N
E
W
S

Mackenzie
Rocky Mountains
Fraser

20
20

St. Lawrence

Ottawa

Land
Tierra

Ocean
Océano

Border
Frontera

Mountain
Montaña

Mexico
México

Río Grande

Sierra Madre Mountains

EL BANCO DE MEXICO $100
50

N
E
W
S

Mexico City

THE NATIVE AMERICANS

Los indígenas americanos

 1. **ceremony**
ceremonia

 11. **pictograph**
pictografía

 2. **mask**
máscara

 12. **loom**
telar

 3. **tepee**
tipi

 13. **weave**
tejer

TOPIC 19

4. **chief**
jefe

 14. **pottery**
cerámica

 5. **tribe**
tribu

 15. **longhouse**
vivienda comunal

 6. **bow**
arco

 16. **hunt**
cazar

 7. **arrow**
flecha

 17. **gather**
recolectar

 8. **spear**
lanza

 18. **grind**
moler

 9. **hide**
piel

 19. **basket**
canasto

 10. **cliff dwelling**
morada en los barrancos

 20. **wampum**
cuentas de conchas

EXPLORATION AND DISCOVERY

Exploración y descubrimientos

 **1. route**
ruta

 **2. Vikings**
vikingos

 **3. Leif Eriksson**
Leif Eriksson

 **4. mast**
mástil

 **5. rope**
cuerda

 6. knot
nudo

 **7. cargo**
carga

 **8. crew**
tripulación

 9. oar
remo

 **10. sailor**
marinero

 **11. prow**
proa

 **12. wave**
ola

 **13. Christopher Columbus**
Cristobal Colón

 **14. Niña**
Niña

 **15. Pinta**
Pinta

 **16. Santa Maria**
Santa María

 17. sail
navegar

 18. jewelry
joyería

 19. native
nativo

 **20. Ponce de León**
Ponce de León

Leif Eriksson

Ponce de León

Christopher Columbus

THE SPANISH MISSIONS
Las misiones españolas

TOPIC 21

1. pueblo
pueblo

2. fort
fuerte

3. trading post
puesto de intercambio

4. adobe
adobe

5. gate
puerta

6. arch
arco

7. patio
patio

8. fountain
fuente

9. cross
cruz

10. bell
campana

11. candles
velas

12. missionary
misionero

13. teach
enseñar

14. Spanish soldiers
soldados españoles

15. ride
montar a caballo

16. sword
espada

San Francisco

Tucson

Santa Fe

St. Augustine

San Diego

San Antonio

COLONIAL LIFE
La vida colonial

1. Pilgrims
peregrinos

9. stockade
empalizada

2. Thanksgiving
Día de Acción de Gracias

10. meetinghouse
salón de reuniones

3. town meeting
asamblea ciudadana

11. courthouse
tribunal de justicia

4. shore
orilla

12. inn
posada

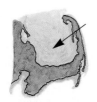

5. bay
bahía

13. mill
molino

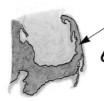

6. cape
cabo

14. blacksmith
herrero

7. harbor
puerto

15. apprentice
aprendiz

8. common
común

16. tobacco
tabaco

TOPIC
22

Maine
(part of Massachusetts)

New
Hampshire

New
York

Massachusetts

Rhode Island

Connecticut

Pennsylvania

New
Jersey

Delaware

Maryland

Virginia

North Carolina

South Carolina

Georgia

THE REVOLUTIONARY WAR

La Guerra Revolucionaria

1. tea
té

2. crate
caja para empacar

3. disguise
disfraz

4. tomahawk
hacha de guerra

5. Paul Revere
Paul Revere

6. Old North Church
Iglesia Old North

7. steeple
campanario

8. lantern
linterna

9. sky
cielo

10. battle
batalla

11. redcoat
casacas rojas

12. Continental soldier
Soldado continental

13. minutemen
miliciano

14. rifle
rifle

15. bayonet
bayoneta

16. musket
mosquete

17. cannon
cañón

18. cannonball
bala de cañón

19. powder horn
cuña de pólvora

20. load
carga

THE BOSTON TEA PARTY

PAUL REVERE'S RIDE

THE BATTLE OF BUNKER HILL

A NATION IS BORN

El nacimiento de una nación

1. Declaration of Independence

Declaración de la Independencia

2. founding fathers

padres fundadores

3. printing press

imprenta

4. printer

impresor

5. pamphlet

panfleto

6. draw

dibujar

7. cartoon

caricatura

8. Benjamin Franklin

Benjamin Franklin

9. write

escribir

10. quill

pluma de ave

11. signature

firma

12. Thomas Jefferson

Thomas Jefferson

13. John Adams

John Adams

14. John Hancock

John Hancock

15. King George III

Rey Jorge III

16. Independence Hall

Edificio de la Independencia

The unanimous Declaration of the thir

WESTWARD EXPANSION

Expansión hacia el Oeste

 **1. flatboat**
barcaza

 **2. steamboat**
barco de vapor

 **3. raft**
balsa

 **4. canoe**
canoa

 **5. canal**
canal

 **6. pioneer**
pionero

 **7. wagon train**
expedición de carretas

 **8. covered wagon**
carreta

 **9. oxen**
bueyes

 **10. pass**
paso

 **11. trail**
sendero

 **12. supplies**
víveres

 13. barrel
barril

 **14. journal**
diario

 **15. homestead**
propiedad

 **16. cabin**
cabaña

 **17. stagecoach**
diligencia

 **18. campsite**
campamento

 **19. trapper**
trampero

 **20. pelt**
piel

TOPIC 25

Westward Expansion
Expansión hacia el Oeste

THE GOLD RUSH
La Fiebre del Oro

TOPIC
26

1. **gold**
oro

2. **Sutter's Mill**
molino de Sutter

3. **prospector**
cateador

4. **pan**
cacerola

5. **dig**
cavar

6. **dirt**
tierra

7. **shovel**
pala

8. **pick**
pico

9. **tent**
tienda

10. **hammer**
martillo

11. **nail**
clavo

12. **Levi Strauss**
Levi Strauss

13. **mule**
mula

14. **clipper ship**
carabela

15. **across**
a través

16. **around**
alrededor

UNIT 3 U.S. HISTORY AND GOVERNMENT
52

THE CIVIL WAR
La Guerra Civil

1. Union
la Unión

2. Yankee
Yanqui

3. Confederacy
Confederación del Sur

4. Rebel
Rebelde

5. Abraham Lincoln
Abraham Lincoln

6. Emancipation Proclamation
Proclamación de Emancipación

7. slave
esclavo

8. flag
bandera

9. knapsack
mochila

10. canteen
cantimplora

11. ammunition
municiones

12. uniform
uniforme

13. cemetery
cementerio

14. surrender
rendirse

15. Ulysses S. Grant
Ulysses S. Grant

16. Robert E. Lee
Robert E. Lee

BULL RUN 1861

GETTYSBURG 1863

APPOMATTOX 1865

U.S. GOVERNMENT
El gobierno de EE.UU.

 **1. Constitution**
Constitución

 **9. Oval Office**
Oficina Oval

 **2. Bill of Rights**
Declaración de Derechos

 10. Great Seal
Emblema

 **3. citizens**
ciudadanos

 **11. legislative branch**
poder legislativo

 **4. candidate**
candidato

 **12. Senate**
Senado

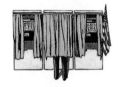 **5. vote**
votar

 **13. House of Representatives**
Cámara de Representante

 6. ballot
boleta

 **14. Congress**
Congreso

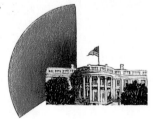 **7. executive branch**
poder ejecutivo

 **15. judicial branch**
poder judicial

 8. President
Presidente

 **16. Supreme Court**
Corte Suprema de Justicia

PEOPLE IN U.S. HISTORY

 1. Pocahontas
1595–1617

 2. George Washington
1731–1799

 3. Sequoya
1760–1843

 4. Sacajawea
1787–1812

 5. Frederick Douglass
1817–1895

 6. Harriet Tubman
1820–1913

 7. Clara Barton
1821–1912

 8. Thomas Edison
1847–1931

 9. Alexander Graham Bell
1847–1922

 10. Susan B. Anthony
1820–1906

 11. Henry Ford
1863–1947

 12. Helen Keller
1880–1968

 13. Eleanor Roosevelt
1884–1962

 14. Margaret Mead
1901–1978

 15. Cesar Chavez
1927–1993

 16. Martin Luther King, Jr.
1929–1968

TOPIC 29

PARTS OF THE BODY
Partes del cuerpo

 1. head
cabeza

 2. hair
cabello

 3. eye
ojo

 4. ear
oreja

 **5. nose**
nariz

 **6. mouth**
boca

 7. teeth
dientes

 8. chin
barbilla

 **9. neck**
cuello

 **10. shoulder**
hombro

 **11. arm**
brazo

 12. elbow
codo

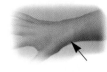 **13. wrist**
muñeca

 14. hand
mano

 **15. finger**
dedo de la mano

 16. thumb
pulgar

 17. chest
pecho

 18. leg
pierna

 **19. knee**
rodilla

 20. ankle
tobillo

 21. foot
pie

22. toe
dedo del pie

TOPIC 30

INSIDE THE HUMAN BODY

Interior del cuerpo humano

1. skeleton
esqueleto

2. bone
hueso

3. skull
cráneo

4. jaw
mandíbula

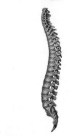

5. spine
espina dorsal

6. muscle
músculo

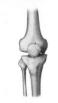

7. joint
articulación

8. cartilage
cartílago

9. ligament
ligamento

10. tendon
tendón

11. brain
cerebro

12. nerve
nervio

13. heart
corazón

14. blood vessels
vasos sanguíneos

15. artery
arteria

16. vein
vena

17. lungs
pulmones

18. esophagus
esófago

19. stomach
estómago

20. intestine
intestino

TOPIC
31

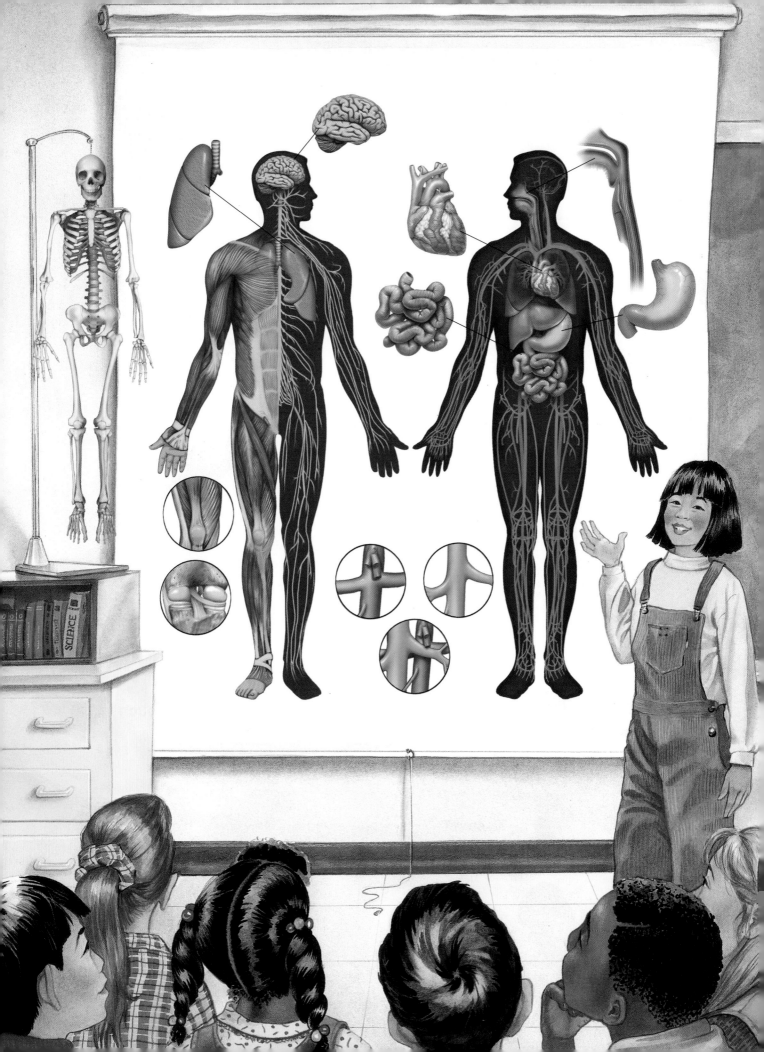

THE SENSES
Los sentidos

 1. **see**
ver

 2. **bright**
brillante

 3. **dark**
oscuro

 4. **hear**
oír

5. **loud**
fuerte

 6. **soft**
suave

 7. **smell**
oler

 8. **fragrant**
aromático

 9. **foul**
fétido

 10. **taste**
saborear

 11. **sweet**
dulce

 12. **sour**
agrio

 13. **salty**
salado

 14. **touch**
tocar

 15. **smooth**
liso

 16. **rough**
áspero

TOPIC 32

FEELINGS
Sensaciones

 1. sick
enfermo

 **2. tired**
cansado

 **3. thirsty**
sediento

 **4. hot**
calor

 5. cold
frío

 **6. hungry**
hambriento

 7. silly
tonto

 **8. shy**
tímido

 9. scared
asustado

 10. surprised
sorprendido

 **11. proud**
orgulloso

 12. sad
triste

 13. happy
feliz

 **14. lonely**
solo

 **15. excited**
emocionado

 **16. angry**
enojado

EXPLORING SCIENCE
Explorar las ciencias

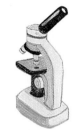 **1. hand lens**
lupa

 **9. eyedropper**
gotero

 2. microscope
microscopio

 **10. fire extinguisher**
extinguidor

 **3. tweezers**
pinzas

 **11. first aid kit**
botiquín de primeros auxilios

 **4. slide**
portaobjetos

 **12. safety glasses**
lentes de seguridad

 5. cover glass
cubreobjetos

 **13. equipment**
equipo

TOPIC 34

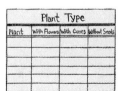 **6. chart**
tabla

 14. model
modelo

 **7. data**
datos

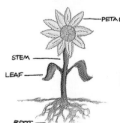 **15. diagram**
diagrama

 **8. collection**
colección

 **16. exhibit**
muestra

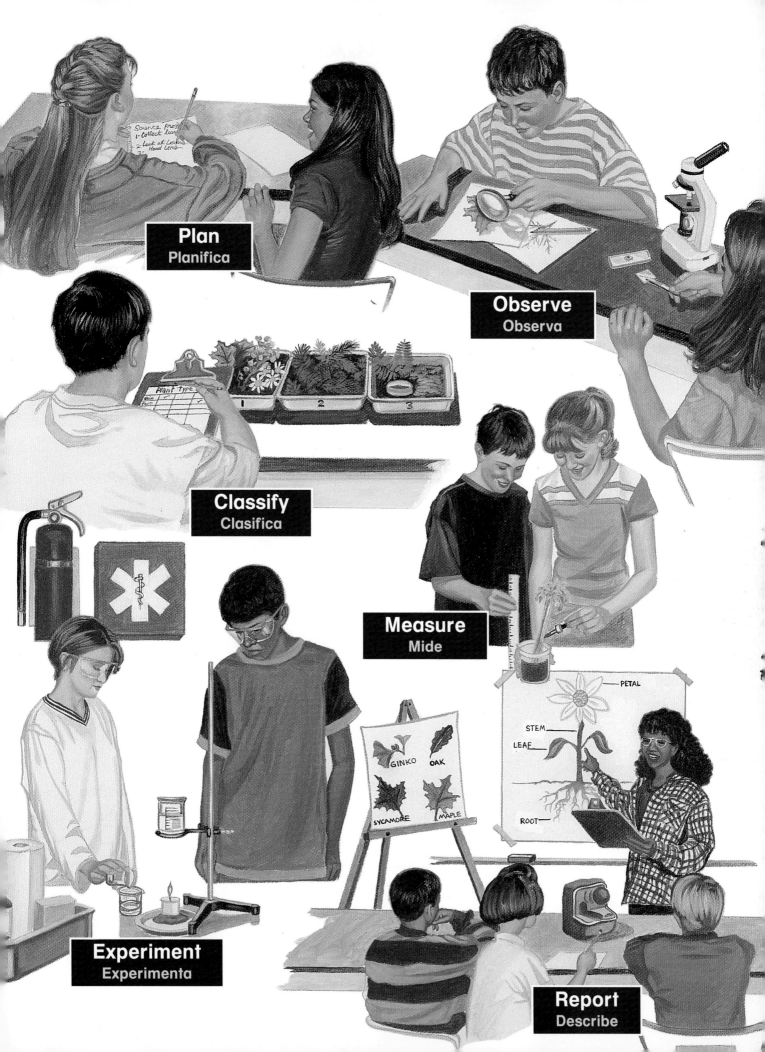

Plan
Planifica

Observe
Observa

Classify
Clasifica

Measure
Mide

Experiment
Experimenta

Report
Describe

GINKO OAK

SYCAMORE MAPLE

PETAL

STEM
LEAF

ROOT

LIVING ORGANISMS

Organismos vivos

 1. plants
plantas

 2. cells
células

 3. cell wall
pared celular

 4. cell membrane
membrana celular

 5. nucleus
núcleo

 6. chromosome
cromosoma

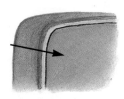 7. cytoplasm
citoplasma

 8. photosynthesis
fotosíntesis

 9. monerans
moneras

 10. protists
prótidos

 11. fungi
hongos

 12. animals
animales

 13. vertebrates
vertebrados

 14. invertebrates
invertebrados

Plants
Plantas

Photosynthesis
Fotosíntesis

Fungi
Hongos

Monerans
Moneras

Protists
Prótidos

Animals
Animales

PLANTS

 1. nut
nuez

 2. seed
semilla

 3. tree
árbol

 4. trunk
tronco

 **5. limb**
rama

 **6. bark**
corteza

 **7. leaf**
hoja

 **8. stem**
tallo

 **9. branch**
rama

 **10. needle**
hoja acicular

 11. pinecone
piña

 12. flower
flor

 13. petal
pétalo

14. stamen
estambre

 15. pistil
pistilo

 16. pollen
polen

 **17. bud**
capullo

 18. stalk
peciolo

 19. bulb
bulbo

 20. root
raíz

VEGETABLES
Verduras

 1. lettuce
lechuga

 2. celery
apio

 3. cabbage
col

 4. broccoli
brócoli

5. cauliflower
coliflor

6. carrot
zanahoria

7. onion
cebolla

 8. radish
rábano

 9. peppers
pimientos

 10. lima beans
habas

 11. cucumber
pepino

 12. string bean
ejote

 13. potato
papa

 14. yam
camote

 15. mushroom
champiñón

 16. peas
guisantes

TOPIC
37

FRUIT
Frutas

 1. banana
plátano

 2. pineapple
piña

 3. cantaloupe
melón

 4. watermelon
sandía

 5. tomato
tomate

 6. peach
durazno

 7. cherry
cereza

 8. avocado
aguacate

 9. pit
semilla

 10. apple
manzana

 11. pear
pera

 12. citrus
cítrico

 13. lemon
limón

 14. lime
lima

 15. orange
naranja

 16. grapefruit
toronja

 17. section
gajo

 18. rind
cáscara

 19. strawberry
fresa

 20. raspberry
frambuesa

SIMPLE ORGANISMS
Organismos simples

 1. amoeba
amiba

 2. paramecium
paramecio

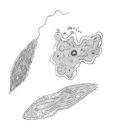 3. protozoans
protozoarios

 4. flatworm
gusano platelminto

 5. roundworm
ascáride

 6. segmented worms
gusanos segmentados

 7. earthworm
lombriz de tierra

 8. leech
sanguijuela

 9. jellyfish
medusa

 10. coral
coral

 11. starfish
estrella de mar

 12. sponge
esponja

 13. sand dollar
erizo de mar aplanado

 14. sea urchin
erizo de mar

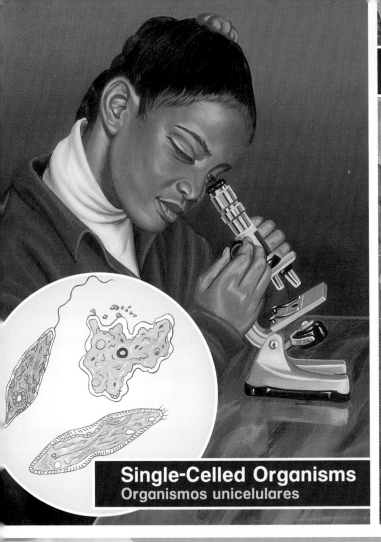

Single-Celled Organisms
Organismos unicelulares

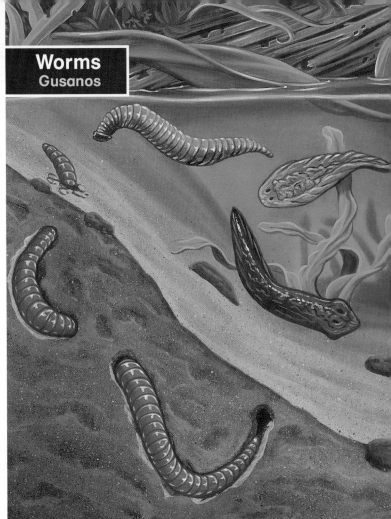

Worms
Gusanos

Sea Creatures
Criaturas marinas

MOLLUSKS AND CRUSTACEANS
Moluscos y crustáceos

1. **octopus**
pulpo

2. **squid**
calamar

3. **tentacles**
tentáculos

4. **sea slug**
babosa de mar

5. **shells**
conchas

6. **scallop**
vieira

7. **clam**
almeja

8. **oyster**
ostión

9. **mussel**
mejillón

10. **conch**
caracola

11. **snail**
caracol

12. **lobster**
langosta

13. **shrimp**
camarón

14. **crab**
cangrejo

15. **claw**
tenaza

16. **antennae**
antenas

17. **barnacles**
percebes

18. **crayfish**
langostino

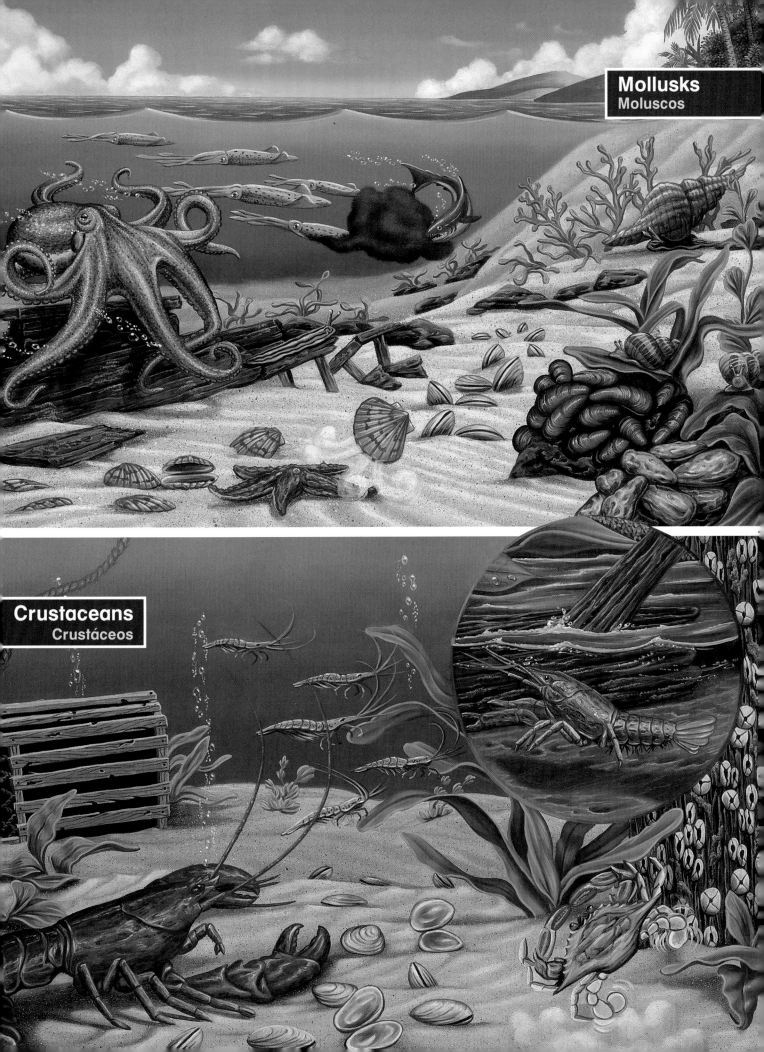

Mollusks
Moluscos

Crustaceans
Crustáceos

INSECTS AND ARACHNIDS

Insectos y arácnidos

 1. **caterpillar**
oruga

 2. **chrysalis**
crisálida

 3. **butterfly**
mariposa

 4. **metamorphosis**
metamorfosis

 5. **hive**
colmena

 6. **bee**
abeja

 7. **ladybug**
catarina

 8. **grasshopper**
saltamontes

 9. **cricket**
grillo

 10. **fly**
mosca

 11. **firefly**
luciérnaga

 12. **mosquito**
mosquito

 13. **ant**
hormiga

 14. **thorax**
tórax

 15. **abdomen**
abdomen

 16. **cockroach**
cucaracha

 17. **spider**
araña

 18. **web**
telaraña

 19. **tick**
garrapata

 20. **scorpion**
escorpión

Insects
Insectos

Arachnids
Arácnidos

FISH

Peces

 1. **bluefish**
pez azul

 10. **fin**
aleta

 2. **swordfish**
pez espada

 11. **gills**
branquias

 3. **shark**
tiburón

 12. **scales**
escamas

 4. **tuna**
atún

 13. **bass**
robalo

 5. **salmon**
salmón

 14. **minnow**
pececillo

 6. **pipefish**
aguja de mar

 15. **trout**
trucha

 7. **eel**
anguila

 16. **perch**
perca

 8. **cod**
bacalao

 17. **catfish**
bagre

 9. **sea horse**
caballito de mar

 18. **goldfish**
pez dorado

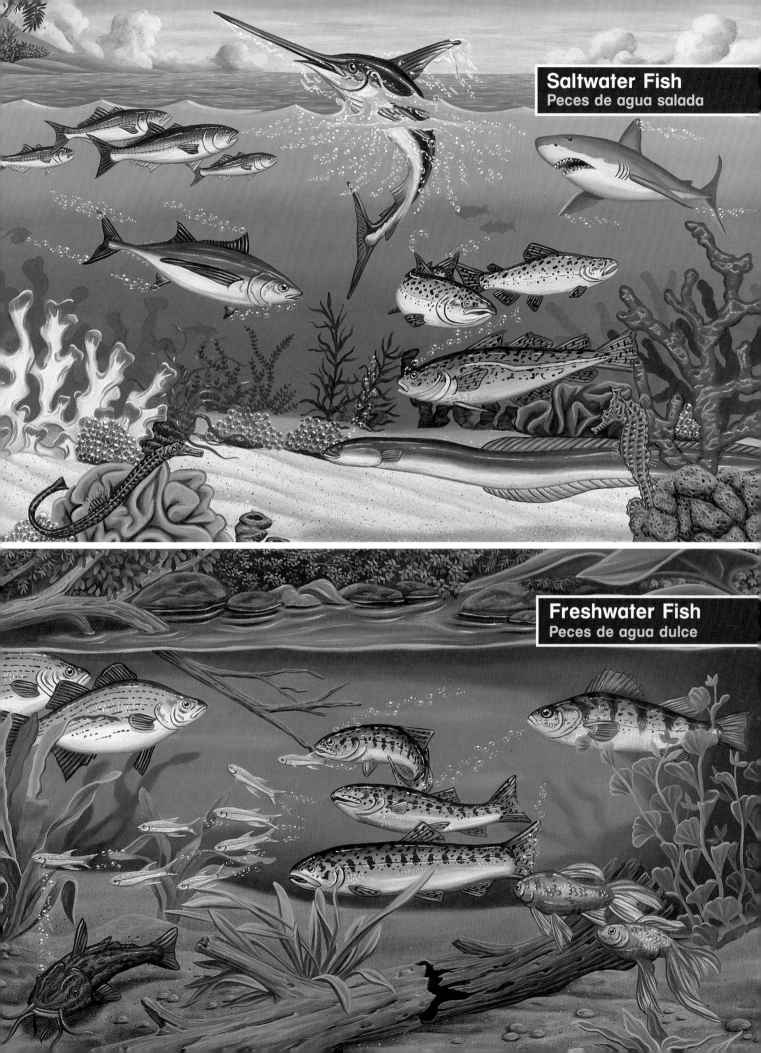

Saltwater Fish
Peces de agua salada

Freshwater Fish
Peces de agua dulce

AMPHIBIANS AND REPTILES

Anfibios y reptiles

1. salamander
salamandra

8. crocodile
cocodrilo

2. tail
cola

9. garter snake
culebra de jaretas

3. frog
rana

10. turtle
tortuga

4. webbed foot
palmípedos

11. chameleon
camaleón

5. tadpole
renacuajo

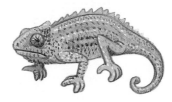

12. iguana
iguana

6. toad
sapo

13. rattlesnake
serpiente de cascabel

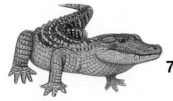

7. alligator
caimán

14. cobra
cobra

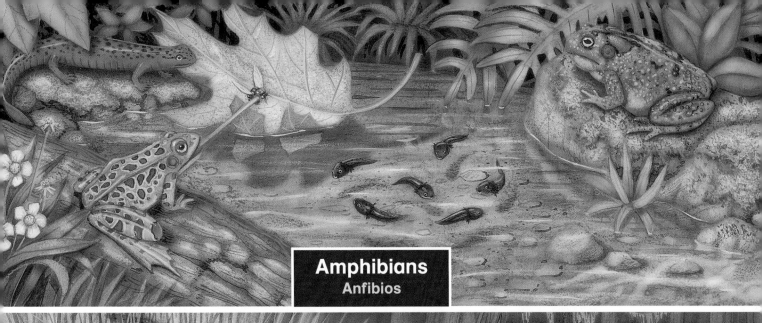

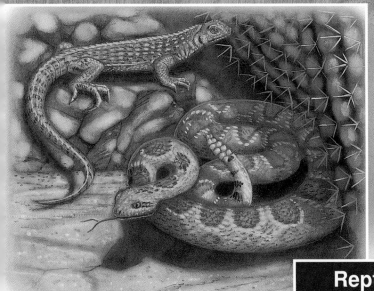

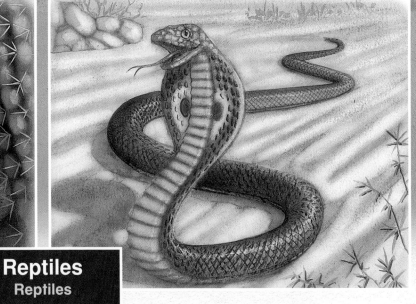

BIRDS
Aves

 1. **pigeon**
paloma

 2. **sparrow**
golondrina

 3. **robin**
petirrojo

 4. **cardinal**
cardenal

 5. **goose**
ganso

 6. **duck**
pato

 7. **hummingbird**
colibrí

 8. **crow**
cuervo

 9. **chicken**
pollo

10. **turkey**
pavo

 11. **seagull**
gaviota

 12. **eagle**
águila

 13. **nest**
nido

 14. **penguin**
pingüino

 15. **ostrich**
avestruz

 16. **peacock**
pavo real

 17. **parrot**
loro

 18. **beak**
pico

 19. **feather**
pluma

 20. **wing**
ala

TOPIC 44

DOMESTIC MAMMALS
Mamíferos domésticos

1. goat
cabra

2. kid
cabrito

3. sheep
oveja

4. lamb
cordero

5. rabbit
conejo

6. bunny
conejito

7. dog
perro

8. puppy
cachorro

9. cow
vaca

10. calf
ternero

11. cat
gato

12. kitten
gatito

13. paw
pata

14. pig
cerdo

15. piglet
cerdito

16. horse
caballo

17. foal
potro

18. forelegs
patas delanteras

19. hind legs
patas traseras

20. hoof
pezuña

WILD MAMMALS
Mamíferos salvajes

 1. squirrel
ardilla

 **2. bat**
murciélago

 3. opossum
zarigüeya

 **4. bear**
oso

 **5. deer**
ciervo

 **6. fur**
piel

 **7. whale**
ballena

 **8. dolphin**
delfín

 **9. camel**
camello

 **10. kangaroo**
canguro

 **11. pouch**
bolsa

 **12. tiger**
tigre

 13. monkey
mono

 **14. giraffe**
jirafa

 **15. lion**
león

 **16. zebra**
cebra

 **17. elephant**
elefante

 **18. tusk**
colmillo

TOPIC 46

PREHISTORIC ANIMALS

Animales prehistóricos

1. dinosaurs
dinosaurios

2. triceratops
triceratops

3. ankylosaurus
anquilosaurio

4. apatosaurus
apatosaurio

5. anatosaurus
anatosaurio

6. diplodocus
diplodocus

7. dryosaurus
driosaurio

8. brachiosaurus
braquiosaurio

9. stegosaurus
estegosaurio

10. spike
púa

11. tyrannosaurus
tiranosaurio

12. pteranodon
pteranodón

13. allosaurus
alosaurio

14. smilodon
smilodonte

15. saber tooth
diente de sable

16. fossil
fósil

TOPIC 47

Herbivores
Herbívoros

Carnivores
Carnívoros

OUR ENVIRONMENT
Problems and Solutions
Nuestro medio ambiente/Problemas y soluciones

 1. **water pollution**
contaminación
del agua

 2. **air pollution**
contaminación
del aire

 3. **soil pollution**
contaminación
del suelo

 4. **smog**
smog

 5. **smoke**
humo

 6. **smokestack**
chimenea

 7. **exhaust**
gases del
tubo de escape

 8. **oil slick**
derrame de petróleo

 9. **litter**
basura

 10. **garbage**
basura

 11. **can**
lata

 12. **bottle**
botella

 13. **landfill**
vertedero

 14. **glass**
vidrio

 15. **plastic**
plástico

 16. **metal**
metal

 17. **compost**
abono orgánico

 18. **carpool**
vehículo compartido

REDUCE!
REUSE!
RECYCLE!

MATTER

La materia

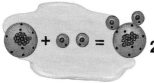 **1. elements**
elementos

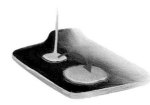 **2. compound**
compuesto

 3. atom
átomo

 4. molecule
molécula

 5. proton
protón

 6. neutron
neutrón

7. electron
electrón

 8. solid
sólido

 **9. liquid**
líquido

 **10. gas**
gas

 **11. physical change**
cambio físico

 12. chemical change
cambio químico

 **13. boil**
hervir

 **14. freeze**
congelar

 **15. melt**
derretir

 **16. evaporate**
evaporar

TOPIC 49

H₂O

Cu 29 Ag 47

ENERGY AND MOTION
Energía y movimiento

 **1. simple machines**
máquinas simples

 **2. axle**
eje

 3. pulley
polea

 4. wheel
rueda

5. wedge
cuña

6. inclined plane
plano inclinado

 **7. lever**
palanca

 8. screw
tornillo

9. magnet
imán

 **10. gears**
engranajes

 11. push
empujar

 12. pull
jalar

 **13. speed**
velocidad

 **14. forces**
fuerzas

 15. friction
fricción

 16. heat
calor

17. light
luz

 18. sound
sonido

TOPIC 50

THE UNIVERSE
El universo

 **1. solar system**
sistema solar

 **10. Saturn**
Saturno

 **2. planets**
planetas

 11. Uranus
Urano

 **3. Sun**
Sol

 12. Neptune
Neptuno

 **4. Moon**
Luna

13. Pluto
Plutón

 5. Mercury
Mercurio

 14. star
estrella

6. Venus
Venus

15. constellation
constelación

 **7. Earth**
Tierra

 **16. meteor**
meteoro

8. Mars
Marte

 **17. comet**
cometa

 9. Jupiter
Júpiter

 **18. galaxy**
galaxia

TOPIC 51

THE EARTH AND ITS LANDFORMS

La Tierra y su topografía

 **1. mountain**
montaña

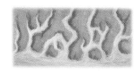 **10. wetland**
tierra pantanosa

 **2. volcano**
volcán

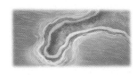 **11. peninsula**
península

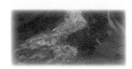 **3. lava**
lava

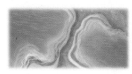 **12. isthmus**
istmo

 **4. plateau**
meseta

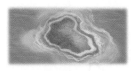 **13. island**
isla

 **5. glacier**
glaciar

 **14. layers**
capas

 **6. valley**
valle

 15. crust
corteza

 **7. river**
río

 16. mantle
manto

 **8. gulf**
golfo

 17. outer core
núcleo externo

 **9. ocean**
océano

 18. inner core
núcleo interno

CLIMATES AND LAND BIOMES
Climas y biomas de tierra

 1. **temperate forest**
bosque templado

 2. **deciduous tree**
árbol deciduo

 3. **taiga**
taiga

 4. **evergreen tree**
árbol de
hojas perennes

 5. **tundra**
tundra

 6. **moss**
musgo

 7. **lichen**
liquen

 8. **tropical rain forest**
bosque tropical

 9. **vines**
enredaderas

 10. **grassland**
sabana

 11. **grass**
pasto

 12. **desert**
desierto

 13. **sand**
arena

 14. **polar zones**
zonas polares

 15. **temperate zones**
zonas templadas

 16. **tropical zone**
zona tropical

TOPIC
53

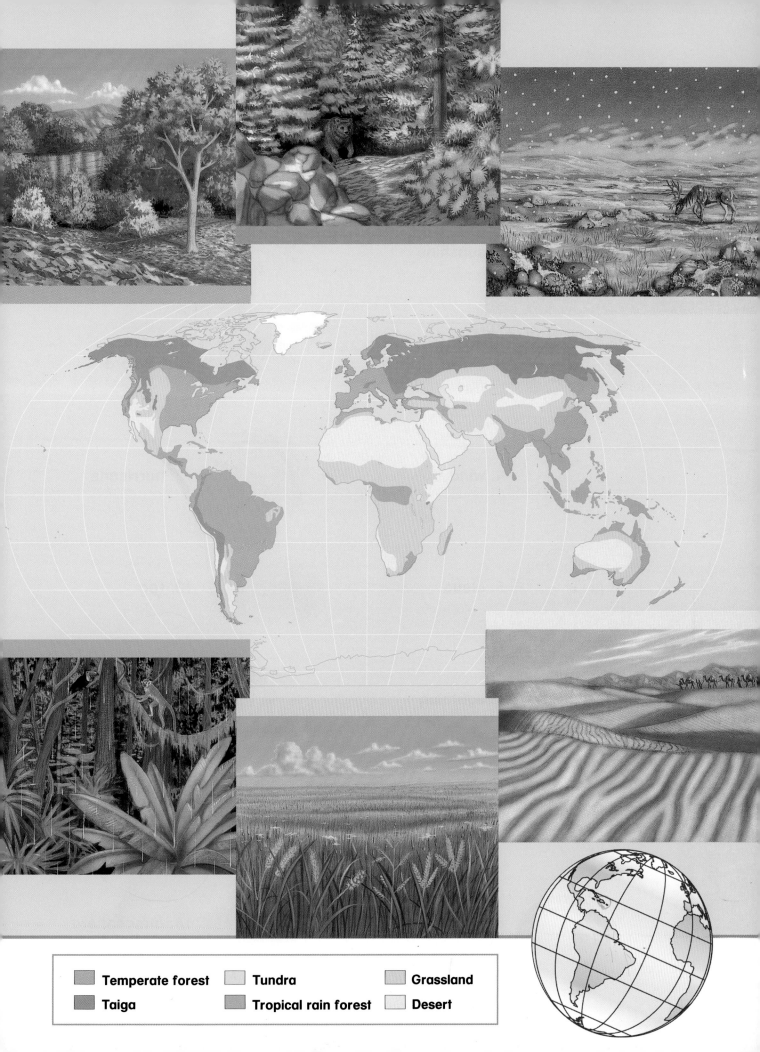

Temperate forest **Tundra** **Grassland**

Taiga **Tropical rain forest** **Desert**

WEATHER

Clima

 **1. forecaster**
meteorólogo

 2. sunshine
luz del sol

 3. snow
nieve

 4. wind
viento

 **5. cloud**
nube

6. lightning
relámpago

 **7. rain**
lluvia

 **8. rainbow**
arco iris

 9. temperature
temperatura

 **10. storms**
tormentas

 **11. blizzard**
ventisca

 **12. hurricane**
huracán

 **13. fog**
neblina

 **14. tornado**
tornado

 **15. sleet**
aguanieve

 **16. atmosphere**
atmósfera

TOPIC 54

EXPLORING MATH

Explorar las matemáticas

-4 -3 -2 -1 0 1 2 3 4   **1. number line**

recta numérica

0123456789   **2. digits**

dígitos

 **3. even numbers**

números pares

 **4. odd numbers**

números impares

+   **5. add**

sumar

$4 + 1 = 5$ **6. sum**

suma

▬   **7. subtract**

restar

$7 - 3 = 4$ **8. difference**

diferencia

 9. multiply

multiplicar

$4 \times 3 = 12$ **10. product**

producto

 11. divide

dividir

$6 \div 3 = 2$ **12. quotient**

cociente

> < =   **13. comparisons**

comparaciones

1   **14. whole number**

número entero

$\frac{1}{2}$ **15. fraction**

fracción

$1\frac{1}{2}$ **16. mixed number**

número mixto

TOPIC 55

GEOMETRY I

Geometría I

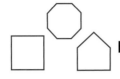 **1. plane figures**
figuras planas

 **10. sphere**
esfera

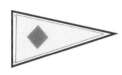 **2. square**
cuadrado

 11. cylinder
cilindro

 3. rectangle
rectángulo

 12. cone
cono

 **4. triangle**
triángulo

 **13. rectangular prism**
prisma rectangular

 **5. circle**
círculo

 14. lines
rectas

 6. pentagon
pentágono

 15. line segment
segmento de recta

 **7. octagon**
octágono

 **16. parallel**
paralelas

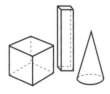 **8. solid figures**
figuras tridimensionales

 17. perpendicular
perpendicular

 9. cube
cubo

 **18. ray**
rayo

TOPIC
56

GEOMETRY II
Geometría II

1. compass
compás

2. circumference
circunferencia

3. diameter
diámetro

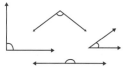

4. angles
ángulos

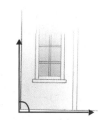

5. right angle
ángulo recto

6. acute angle
ángulo agudo

7. obtuse angle
ángulo obtuso

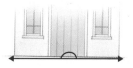

8. straight angle
ángulo plano

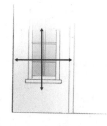

9. intersecting lines
rectas secantes

10. perimeter
perímetro

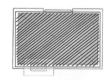

11. area
área

12. height
altura

13. length
longitud

14. width
ancho

15. base
base

16. edge
arista

17. symmetrical
simétrico

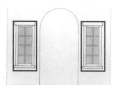

18. congruent figures
figuras congruentes

TOPIC
57

MEASUREMENT

Medidas

1. centimeter
centímetro

10. ton
tonelada

2. meter
metro

11. mile
milla

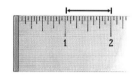
3. inch
pulgada

12. teaspoon
cucharadita

4. foot
pie

13. tablespoon
cucharada

5. weight
peso

14. cup
taza

6. gram
gramo

15. liter
litro

7. kilogram
kilogramo

16. pint
pinta

8. ounce
onza

17. quart
cuarto de galón

9. pound
libra

18. gallon
galón

FABRICS

1 TON

FIRST BANK OF A

1 2 3

1 2 3 4 5 6 7 8 9 10 11 12 13

ICE CREAM

GEMS &
JEWELRY

1 LB. 2 OZ.

1 qt. 1 qt. 1 qt. 1 qt. 1 pt. 1 pt. 1 pt.

1 gal. 1 gal. 1 gal. 1 pt. 1 pt.

1 ℓ. 1 ℓ. 1 ℓ.

T. t. 1 ℓ.

NUMBER PATTERNS, FUNCTIONS, AND RELATIONS

Patrones numéricos, funciones y relaciones

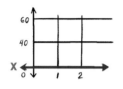 **1. graphs**
gráficas

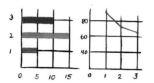 **8. random order**
orden aleatorio

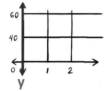 **2. x-axis**
eje x

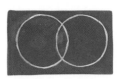 **9. Venn diagram**
diagrama de Venn

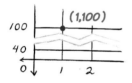 **3. y-axis**
eje y

10. table
tabla

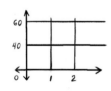 **4. coordinates**
coordenadas

 **11. chart**
cuadro

5. coordinate plane
plano de coordenadas

 **12. sequence**
secuencia

 6. ascending order
orden ascendente

 **13. finite set**
conjunto finito

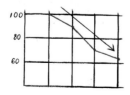 **7. descending order**
orden descendente

 **14. infinite set**
conjunto infinito

COMPUTERS AND CALCULATORS

Computadoras y calculadoras

1. personal computer (PC)
computadora personal

2. monitor
monitor

3. cursor
cursor

4. keyboard
teclado

5. mouse
ratón

6. disk drive
unidad de disco

7. diskette
disquete

8. compact disc (CD)
disco compacto (CD)

9. switch
interruptor

10. cable
cable

11. power supply
fuente de energía

12. display
pantalla

13. operations keys
teclas de operaciones

14. equals key
tecla de igualdad

15. unit key
tecla de unidad

16. fraction bar
tecla de división

17. percent key
tecla de porcentaje

18. clear key
tecla de reinicio

19. decimal point key
tecla de punto decimal

20. memory recall
tecla de memoria

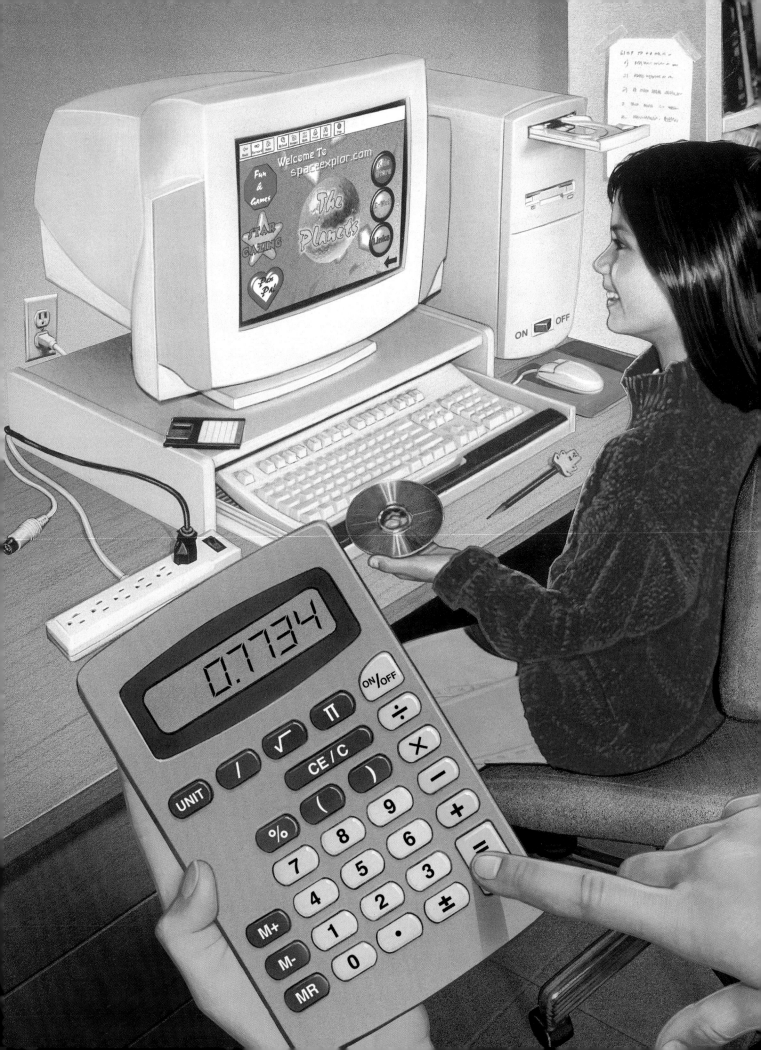

NUMBERS
Números

0	zero / cero	**13**	thirteen / trece	**30**	thirty / treinta
1	one / uno	**14**	fourteen / catorce	**40**	forty / cuarenta
2	two / dos	**15**	fifteen / quince	**50**	fifty / cincuenta
3	three / tres	**16**	sixteen / dieciséis	**60**	sixty / sesenta
4	four / cuatro	**17**	seventeen / diecisiete	**70**	seventy / setenta
5	five / cinco	**18**	eighteen / dieciocho	**80**	eighty / ochenta
6	six / seis	**19**	nineteen / diecinueve	**90**	ninety / noventa
7	seven / siete	**20**	twenty / veinte	**100**	one hundred / cien
8	eight / ocho	**21**	twenty-one / veintiuno	**500**	five hundred / quinientos
9	nine / nueve	**22**	twenty-two / veintidós		
10	ten / diez	**23**	twenty-three / veintitrés	**1,000**	one thousand / mil
11	eleven / once	**24**	twenty-four / veinticuatro	**1,000,000**	one million / un millón
12	twelve / doce	**25**	twenty-five / veinticinco		

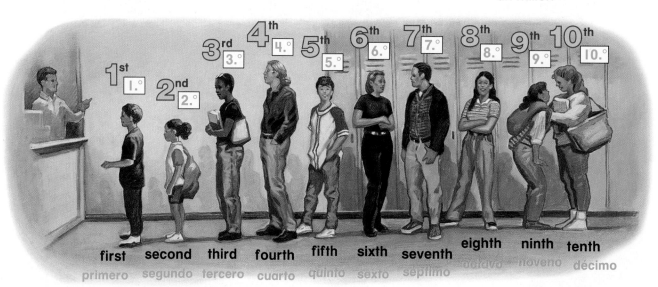

1st 1.° first / primero
2nd 2.° second / segundo
3rd 3.° third / tercero
4th 4.° fourth / cuarto
5th 5.° fifth / quinto
6th 6.° sixth / sexto
7th 7.° seventh / séptimo
8th 8.° eighth / octavo
9th 9.° ninth / noveno
10th 10.° tenth / décimo

TIME
La hora

Day Día

morning
mañana

noon
mediodía

afternoon
tarde

Night Noche

evening
tarde

midnight
medianoche

MONEY
Dinero

bills
billetes

dollar
dólar

quarter
moneda
de 25¢

nickel
moneda
de 5¢

penny
moneda
de 1¢

dime
moneda
de 10¢

coins
monedas

THE CALENDAR
El calendario

SUN	MON	TUE	WED	THUR	FRI	SAT
1	2	3	4	5	6	7
8	9	10	11	12	13	14
15	16	17	18	19	20	21
22	23	24	25	26	27	28
29	30	31				

Months
Meses

January enero	**February** febrero
March marzo	**April** abril
May mayo	**June** junio
July julio	**August** agosto
September septiembre	**October** octubre
November noviembre	**December** diciembre

The Days of the Week Los días de la semana

Sunday domingo	**Monday** lunes	**Tuesday** martes	**Wednesday** miércoles	**Thursday** jueves	**Friday** viernes	**Saturday** sábado

COLORS Colores

red rojo	**yellow** amarillo	**blue** azul	**orange** anaranjado	**green** verde	**purple** morado
brown café	**pink** rosado	**tan** canela	**gray** gris	**white** blanco	**black** negro

OPPOSITES

Antónimos

large
grande

small
pequeño

left
izquierda

right
derecha

tall
alto

short
bajo

thick
grueso

thin
delgado

high
alto

low
bajo

empty
vacío

full
lleno

open
abierto

closed
cerrado

old
viejo

new
nuevo

dirty
sucio

clean
limpio

FOOD
Alimentos

Breakfast
Desayuno

syrup
sirope

eggs
huevos

pancakes
panqueques

bacon
tocino

milk
leche

toast
pan tostado

juice
jugo

honey
miel

butter
mantequilla

cereal
cereal

Lunch
Almuerzo

sandwich
sándwich

pizza
pizza

mustard
mostaza

hot dog
perrito caliente

cheese
queso

salad
ensalada

pudding
budín

soup
sopa

cake
pastel

ketchup
salsa catsup

french fries
papas fritas

hamburger
hamburguesa

Dinner
Cena

pepper
pimienta

pie
tarta

salt
sal

fruit salad
ensalada
de frutas

pasta
pasta

mashed potatoes
puré de papas

meat
carne

asparagus
espárragos

Snacks
Antojitos

peanut butter
mantequilla de
cacahuate

popcorn
palomitas

jelly
mermelada

yogurt
yogur

cookies
galletas

bread
pan

peanuts
cacahuates

ice cream
helado

CLOTHING
Ropa

raincoat
gabardina

ski cap
pasamontañas

scarf
bufanda

jacket
chaqueta

baseball cap
gorra de béisbol

sweatshirt
sudadera

T-shirt
camiseta

gloves
guantes

mittens
manoplas

jeans
pantalones
de mezclilla

sweater
suéter

boots
botas

sneakers
tenis

sweatpants
sudadera

dress
vestido

earrings
aretes

shirt
camisa

bathrobe
bata

pajamas
piyama

blouse
blusa

tie
corbata

coat
abrigo

ring
anillo

skirt
falda

belt
cinturón

bracelet
brazalete

suit
traje

pants
pantalones

shorts
pantalones cortos

underwear
ropa interior

tights
pantimedias

slippers
pantuflas

nightgown
camisón
de dormir

underpants
calzoncillos

shoes
zapatos

socks
calcetines

WORLD MAP
Mapamundi

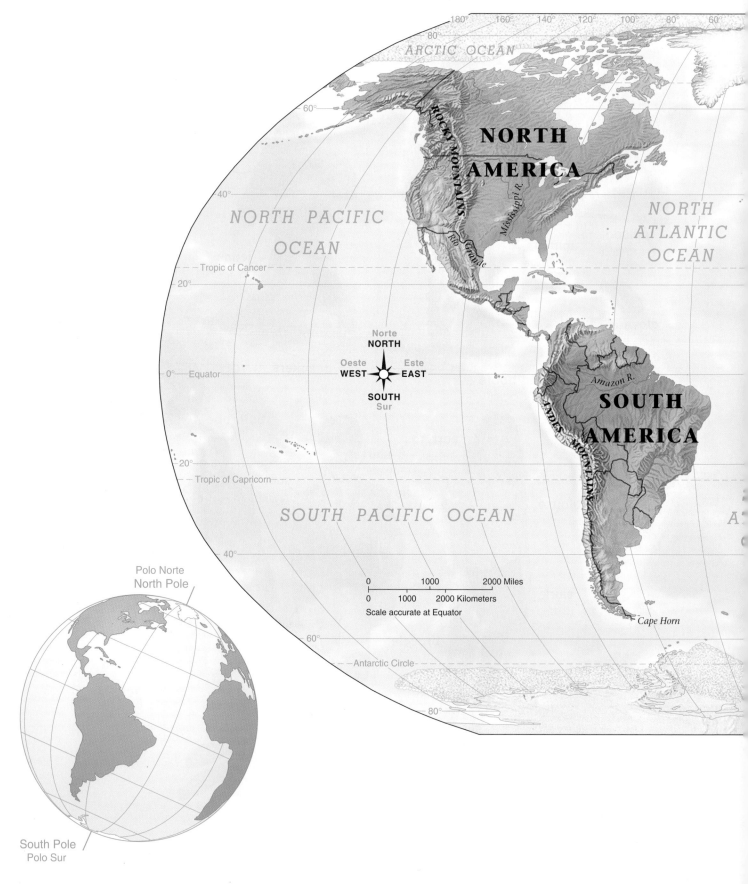

ARCTIC OCEAN

NORTH
AMERICA

ROCKY MOUNTAINS

Mississippi R.

Rio Grande

NORTH PACIFIC
OCEAN

NORTH
ATLANTIC
OCEAN

Tropic of Cancer

Norte
NORTH
Oeste   Este
WEST   EAST
SOUTH
Sur

Equator

Amazon R.

SOUTH
AMERICA

ANDES MOUNTAINS

Tropic of Capricorn

SOUTH PACIFIC OCEAN

0   1000   2000 Miles
0   1000   2000 Kilometers
Scale accurate at Equator

Cape Horn

Polo Norte
North Pole

Antarctic Circle

South Pole
Polo Sur

ARCTIC OCEAN

EUROPE

ALPS

URAL MTS.

Volga R.

Ob R.

ASIA

ATLAS MTS.

Nile R.

Indus R.

HIMALAYAS

Yangtze R.

Niger R.

AFRICA

PACIFIC OCEAN

INDIAN OCEAN

AUSTRALIA

Cape of
Good Hope

IC

ANTARCTICA

WORD LIST

The numbers to the right of the entries indicate the page on which the word is introduced. Words in black are the content words found in the illustration. Words in pink appear in a topic's title or can be found as labels or text within a topic's main illustration.

A

abdomen **82**
across **52**
actor **34**
actress **34**
acute angle **114**
Adams, John **48**
add **110**
adobe **42**
advertisement **22**
Africa **128–129**
afternoon **123**
agriculture **26**
air pollution **96**
airplane **14**
Alabama **20**
Alaska **20**
Alaska Pipeline **30**
alligator **86**
allosaurus **94**
ambulance **16**
American Samoa **20**
ammunition **54**
amoeba **78**
amphibians **86**
anatosaurus **94**
angles **114**
angry **66**
animals **70**
ankle **60**
ankylosaurus **94**
ant **82**
Antarctica **128–129**
antennae **80**
Anthony, Susan B. **58**
apartment building **10**
apatosaurus **94**
apple **76**
Appomattox **55**
apprentice **44**
April **124**
arachnids **82**

arch **42**
Arctic Ocean **128–129**
area **114**
Arizona **20**
Arkansas **20**
arm **60**
around **52**
arrow **38**
artery **62**
ascending order **118**
Asia **128–129**
asparagus **126**
assembly line **24**
Atlantic Ocean **128–129**
atmosphere **108**
atom **98**
attic **6**
auditorium **4**
August **124**
aunt **8**
Australia **128–129**
avocado **76**
axle **100**

B

baby **8**
bacon **126**
ballot **56**
banana **76**
bandage **16**
bank **10**
bark **72**
barn **14**
barnacles **80**
barrel **50**
Barton, Clara **58**
base **114**
baseball cap **127**
basement **6**
basket **38**
basketball **12**
bass **84**

bat **92**
bathrobe **127**
bathroom **6**
bathtub **6**
battle **46**
bay **44**
bayonet **46**
beak **88**
bear **92**
beautiful **33**
bed **16**
bedroom **6**
bee **82**
bell **42**
Bell, Alexander Graham **58**
belt **127**
bicycle **12**
Bill of Rights **56**
bills **123**
birds **88**
black **124**
blacksmith **44**
blanket **16**
blizzard **108**
block **12**
blood vessels **62**
blouse **127**
blue **124**
bluefish **84**
boat **30**
body **60**
boil **98**
bone **62**
book **2**
boots **127**
born **48**
both **119**
bottle **96**
bow **38**
boys room **4**
bracelet **127**
brachiosaurus **94**
brain **62**

headline **22**
hear **64**
heart **62**
heat **100**
height **114**
helicopter **10**
herbivores **95**
herd **28**
hide **38**
high **125**
hills **14**
hind legs **90**
hive **82**
homestead **50**
honey **126**
hoof **90**
horse **90**
hospital **16**
hot **66**
hot dog **126**
hotel **10**
hours **123**
house **6**
House of Representatives **56**
hummingbird **88**
hungry **66**
hunt **38**
hurricane **108**
hydroelectric plant **32**

I

ice cream **126**
Idaho **20**
iguana **86**
Illinois **20**
inch **116**
inclined plane **100**
Independence Hall **48**
Indian Ocean **128–129**
Indiana **20**
infinite set **118**
information **112**
inn **44**
insects **82**
intersecting lines **114**
intestine **62**
invertebrates **70**
Iowa **20**
irrigation canal **32**

island **104**
isthmus **104**

J

jacket **127**
January **124**
jaw **62**
jeans **127**
Jefferson, Thomas **48**
jelly **126**
jellyfish **78**
jewelry **40**
joint **62**
journal **50**
judicial branch **56**
juice **126**
July **124**
June **124**
jungle **106**
Jupiter **102**

K

kangaroo **92**
Kansas **20**
Keller, Helen **58**
Kennedy Space Center **24**
Kentucky **20**
ketchup **126**
keyboard **120**
kid **90**
kilogram **116**
King George III **48**
King, Martin Luther Jr. **58**
kitchen **6**
kitten **90**
knapsack **54**
knee **60**
knot **40**

L

ladybug **82**
lamb **90**
land biomes **106**
landfill **96**
landforms **104**
lantern **46**

large **125**
laser **34**
latitude **36**
lava **104**
layers **104**
leaf **72**
Lee, Robert E. **54**
leech **78**
left **125**
leg **60**
legend **36**
legislative branch **56**
Leif Eriksson **40**
lemon **76**
length **114**
lettuce **74**
lever **100**
Liberty Bell **22**
librarian **4**
library **4**
lichen **106**
ligament **62**
light **100**
lightning **108**
lima beans **74**
limb **72**
lime **76**
Lincoln, Abraham **54**
line segment **112**
lines **112**
lion **92**
liquid **98**
liter **116**
litter **96**
livestock **28**
living **70**
living room **6**
load **46**
lobster **80**
locker **4**
logging **30**
lonely **66**
longhouse **38**
longitude **36**
loom **38**
loud **64**
Louisiana **20**
low **125**
lumber **24**
lumberjack **30**

O

oar 40
observe 69
obtuse angle 114
ocean 104
octagon 112
October 124
octopus 80
odd numbers 110
office 4
office building 10
Ohio 20
oil 32
oil slick 96
Oklahoma 20
old 125
Old Faithful 28
Old North Church 46
one 122
one hundred 122
one million 122
one thousand 122
onion 74
open 125
open pit 28
operations keys 120
opossum 92
opposites 125
orange 124
orange 76
orchard 14
ore 28
Oregon 20
organisms, single-celled 79
organisms 70
ostrich 88
Ottawa 37
ounce 116
Oval Office 56
overhead projector 2
oxen 50
oyster 80

P

Pacific 34
Pacific Ocean 128–129
painter 18
pajamas 127

pamphlet 48
pan 52
pancakes 126
pants 127
paper 2
parallel 112
paramecium 78
paramedic 16
parents 8
park 12
parking garage 10
parrot 88
pass 50
pasta 126
pasture 14
path 14
patient 16
patio 42
paw 90
peach 76
peacock 88
peak 28
peanut butter 126
peanuts 126
pear 76
peas 74
pelt 50
pen 2
pencil 2
pencil sharpener 2
penguin 88
peninsula 104
Pennsylvania 20
penny 123
pentagon 112
pepper 126
peppers 74
percent key 120
perch 84
perimeter 114
perpendicular 112
personal computer (PC) 120
petal 72
pharmacist 18
photosynthesis 70
physical change 98
pick 52
pictograph 38
pie 126
pig 90

pigeon 88
piglet 90
Pilgrims 44
pillow 16
pine 30
pineapple 76
pinecone 72
pink 124
pint 116
Pinta 40
pioneer 50
pipefish 84
pipeline 32
pistil 72
pit 76
pizza 126
plan 69
plane figures 112
planets 102
plantation 24
plant (v.) 26
plants 70
plastic 96
plateau 104
playground 4
plow 26
plumber 18
Pluto 102
Pocahontas 58
polar zones 106
police officer 18
police station 10
pollen 72
pollution (see air, soil, water) 96
Ponce de León 40
pond 14
popcorn 126
porch 6
port 24
post office 10
potato 74
pottery 38
pouch 92
pound 116
powder horn 46
power supply 120
prehistoric animals 94
President 56
principal 4
printer 48

White House, The   22
whole number   110
width   114
wind   108
window   6
wing   88
Wisconsin   20
wood   30
woods   14
work   18
worker   24
World   128–129
worms   79
wrist   60
write   48
writer   18
Wyoming   20

X

x-axis   118
X ray   16

Y

y-axis   118
yam   74
Yankee   54
yard   12
yellow   124
Yellowstone National Park   28
yogurt   126

Z

zebra   92
zero   122

LISTA DE PALABRAS

Los números indican la página donde aparecen las palabras. Las palabras en negro son las de contenido, y están relacionadas con las ilustraciones. Las palabras en rosa aparecen en los títulos de los temas, o pueden aparecer en los rótulos de las ilustraciones principales.

A

a través **52**
abdomen **82**
abeja **82**
abierto **125**
abono orgánico **96**
abrigo **127**
abril **124**
abuela **8**
abuelo **8**
abuelos **8**
acciones y bonos **22**
acera **12**
actor **34**
actriz **34**
Adams, John **48**
adobe **42**
África **128-129**
agosto **124**
agricultura **26**
agrio **64**
aguacate **76**
aguanieve **108**
águila **88**
aguja de mar **84**
Aguja Espacial **30**
ala **88**
Alabama **20**
alacena **6**
Alaska **20**
alberca **12**
aleta **84**
algodón **24**
alimentos **126**
almeja **80**
almohada **16**
almuerzo **126**
alosaurio **94**
alrededor **52**
alto **125**
altura **114**
amarillo **124**
ambulancia **16**
amiba **78**
anaranjado **76**
anatosaurio **94**
ancho **114**
anfibios **86**
anguila **84**
ángulo agudo **114**
ángulo obtuso **114**
ángulo plano **114**
ángulo recto **114**
ángulos **114**
anillo **127**

animales **70**
animales prehistóricos **94**
anquilosaurio **94**
Antártida **128-129**
antenas **80**
Anthony, Susan B. **58**
antojitos **126**
antónimos **125**
anuncio **22**
apatosaurio **94**
apio **74**
Appomattox **55**
aprendiz **44**
arácnidos **82**
arado **26**
araña **82**
árbol **72**
árbol de hojas perennes **106**
árbol deciduo **106**
árboles maderables **30**
arco (y flecha) **38**
arco (arquitectura) **42**
arco iris **108**
ardilla **92**
área **114**
arena **106**
aretes **127**
arista **114**
Arizona **20**
Arkansas **20**
armario (lócker) **4**
armario (clóset) **6**
aromático **64**
arroyo **14**
arroz **24**
arteria **62**
articulación **62**
asamblea ciudadana **44**
ascáride **78**
aserradero **30**
aserrín **30**
Asia **128-129**
áspero **64**
asustado **66**
ático **6**
atmósfera **108**
átomo **98**
atún **84**
auditorio **4**
Australia **128-129**
autobús **10**
autopista **34**
aves **88**
avestruz **88**
avión **14**
ayudante de dentista **18**

azúcar **24**
azul **124**

B

babosa de mar **80**
bacalao **84**
bagre **84**
bahía **44**
bajo **125**
bala de cañón **50**
ballena **26**
balsa **50**
banco **10**
bandera **54**
bañera **6**
baño **6**
barbilla **60**
barcaza **50**
barco de vapor **50**
barril **50**
barrios periféricos **12**
Barton, Clara **58**
base **114**
básquetbol **12**
basura **96**
bata **127**
batalla **46**
bayoneta **46**
bebé **8**
bebedero **4**
Bell, Alexander Graham **58**
biblioteca **4**
bibliotecario **4**
bicicleta **12**
billetes **123**
biomas de tierra **106**
bisonte **28**
blanco **22**
blusa **127**
boca **60**
boleta **56**
bolsa **92**
bombero **18**
bosque **14, 30**
bosque templado **106**
bosque tropical **106**
botas **127**
bote **30**
botella **96**
botiquín de primeros auxilios **68**
branquias **84**
braquiosaurio **94**
brazalete **127**
brazo **60**
brillante **64**
brócoli **74**